Not All Birds Fly

written by Jaclyn Crupi

Engage Literacy is published in 2013 by Raintree.
Raintree is an imprint of Capstone Global Library Limited, a company incorporated in Engand and Wales having its registered office at 7 Pilgrim Street, London, EC4V 6LB – Registered company number: 6695582
www.raintreepublishers.co.uk

Originally published in Australia by Hinkler Education, a division of Hinkler Books Pty Ltd.
Text and illustration copyright © Hinkler Books Pty Ltd 2012

Written by Jaclyn Crupi
Lead authors Jay Dale and Anne Giulieri
Illustrations pp 10, 11, 13, 15, 17–20, 22, 24 by Gaston Vanzet
Edited by Gwenda Smyth
UK edition edited by Dan Nunn, Catherine Veitch and Sian Smith
Designed by Susannah Low, Butterflyrocket Design

All rights reserved. No part of this publication may be reproduced, stored in a retrieval system, or transmitted in any way or by any means, electronic, mechanical, photocopying, recording or otherwise, without the prior written permission of Capstone Global Library Limited.

Not All Birds Fly
ISBN: 978 1 406 26541 5
10 9 8 7 6 5 4 3 2 1

Printed and bound in China by Leo Paper Products Ltd

Acknowledgements
Cover (and title page) image by © Jan Martin Will | Dreamstime.com; p4 left: © Jan Martin Will | Dreamstime.com; p4 right: © Javarman | Dreamstime.com; p5 left: © NHPA/David Tipling; p5 right: © Sgoodwin4813 | Dreamstime.com; p6 left: © NHPA/Gerald Cubitt; p6 right: © Christian Degroote | Dreamstime.com; p7 top: Stocktrek Images/SuperStock; p7 bottom: iStockphoto.com/ © Marshall Bruce; p8 top left: © Jan Martin Will | Dreamstime.com; p8 top middle: © Michel Sauret | Dreamstime.com; p8 top right: © NHPA/Ann & Steve Toon; p8 bottom left: © Gentoomultimedia | Dreamstime.com; p8 bottom right (and Contents page): © Joshanon1 | Dreamstime.com; p9 top left: © Javarman | Dreamstime.com; p9 top middle left: iStockphoto.com/ © Jan Will; p9 top middle right: iStockphoto.com/ © MOF; p9 top right: © Andybignellphoto | Dreamstime.com; p9 middle: © Michael Elliott | Dreamstime.com; p9 bottom left: © Christian Musat; p9 bottom right: iStockphoto.com/ © Island Effects; p11 top: © Vladimir Seliverstov | Dreamstime.com; p12 left: © NHPA/Joe Blossom; p12 right: iStockphoto.com/ © John Carnemolla; p14: © Steven David Miller/AUSCAPE; p15: © Dave Watts/AUSCAPE; p16 top: Minden Pictures/SuperStock; p16 bottom: © Tui De Roy/AUSCAPE; p18 bottom right: © NHPA/ A.N.T. Photo Library; p19 top: JTB Photo Communicati / JTB Photo/SuperStock; p20 top: © Ferrero- Labat/AUSCAPE; p20 middle (and back cover and Contents page): iStockphoto.com/ © David Gomez; p21 bottom: © M&C Denis-Huot -BIOS /AUSCAPE; p22 top: © Hiroshi KOMIYAMA-Nature Production/AUSCAPE; p23 top left: © Johannes Gerhardus Swanepoel | Dreamstime.com; p23 middle right: © Steve Allen | Dreamstime.com; p23 bottom left: Steve Vidler/SuperStock; p23 bottom right: © Dean Bertoncelj | Dreamstime.com

Contents

Why Don't Some Birds Fly?	4
Penguins	8
Emus	12
Kiwis	16
Ostriches	20
Picture Glossary	24

Why Don't Some Birds Fly?

When we think about birds,
we often think about them
spreading their wings,
and flying high in the sky.
All birds can fly. Isn't that right?
Well, the answer to this question is 'no'.
Not **all** birds can fly.

Emperor penguins

Gentoo penguins

Flightless duck

Emu

Over many thousands of years, some birds became very good swimmers or runners. That meant they didn't need their wings to fly away from their *enemies* — they could either run or swim to get away. Their wings weren't used for flying anymore.

Kiwi

Ostrich

DID YOU KNOW?

Many scientists believe that millions of years ago, birds were a kind of dinosaur. Some even think there were dinosaurs with feathers.

WORD FACT

An enemy is something or someone that makes you feel unsafe. A bird's enemy is usually another animal that wants to eat it. Another word for this is predator.

 Emperor
 Macaroni
 Fairy

Penguins

The penguin is a bird that cannot fly.
There are many different kinds of penguins.

Many penguins live in Antarctica.
They live in the water, and on snow and ice.
A penguin spends about the same amount
of time in the ocean as it does on land.

 Gentoo
 King
 Adelie
 Rockhopper

Penguins have short feathers that overlap and cover their body. This helps to keep them warm.

Penguins use their wings like flippers and these are perfect for swimming.

Penguins have white fronts and black backs.
This helps to keep them safe from their enemies.
They can also bite to protect themselves.

DID YOU KNOW?

Penguins sometimes take a nap while in the water.

The female penguin hunts for food
while the male looks after their egg.
When the female comes back,
it is the male's turn to look for food.
When the chick hatches,
it calls to its parents straightaway.
This is so the parents know the sound
of its voice and can easily find their chick.

FAST FACTS

Name: penguin
Habitat: ocean, ice, snow, rocks
Diet: squid, fish, *krill*
Predators: sea lions, seals, foxes, even cats!
Where found: Antarctica and other parts of the Southern Hemisphere

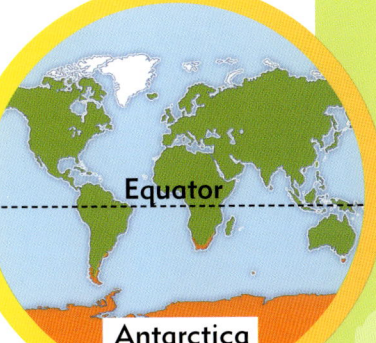

Emus

The emu is an Australian animal. It is the second largest bird in the world. It has a long, thin neck and long, thin legs. Emus are very tall birds that cannot fly but can run very fast.

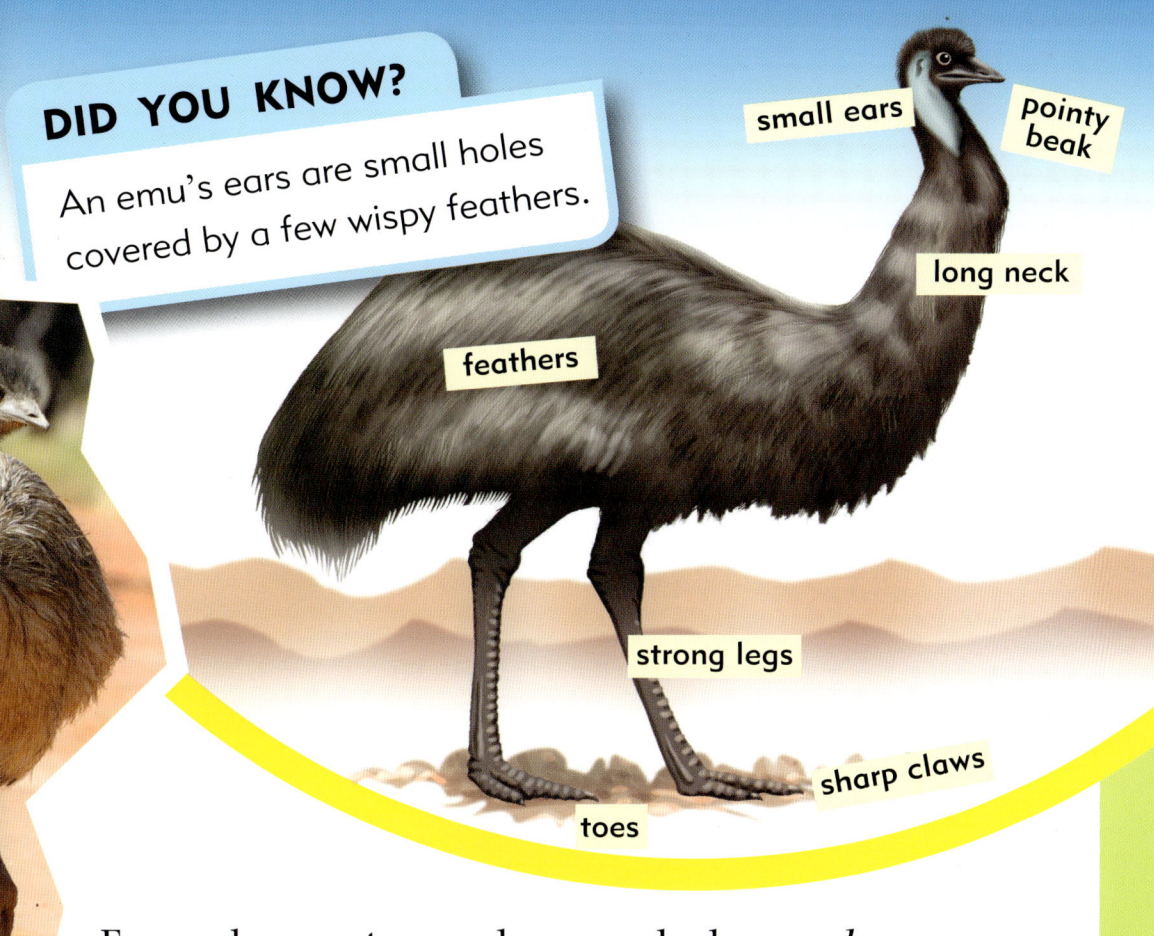

DID YOU KNOW?
An emu's ears are small holes covered by a few wispy feathers.

small ears
pointy beak
long neck
feathers
strong legs
sharp claws
toes

Emus have strong legs and sharp *claws* on their toes.
These claws can be very dangerous when an emu kicks out at its enemies.
Emus also have stiff tail feathers.
When they want to scare their enemies away, they shake or rattle their stiff tail feathers.

Emus use *camouflage* to keep them safe from their enemies. Their feathers are often a similar colour to the grass and trees around them.
Emus have excellent eyesight and hearing.
This also helps to keep them safe from their enemies.

DID YOU KNOW?

The male emu builds a nest from sticks, leaves, bark and grass in a *hollow* in the ground. Once the female lays her eggs, the male sits on them and waits for them to hatch.

FAST FACTS

Name: emu
Habitat: grasslands
Diet: fruit, flowers, insects, seeds, green plants
Predators: lizards, *dingoes*, eagles, cats, dogs, foxes
Where found: Australia

Kiwis

Kiwis are birds from New Zealand. They are the smallest of all the birds that cannot fly. Kiwis have tiny wings that are very difficult to see. They have a small body and a very long beak. Kiwis are the only birds with *nostrils* at the end of their beak. They use their excellent sense of smell and their beak to find insects and worms underground. They are very shy animals and are most active at night. Animals that are active at night are called nocturnal animals.

Like some other birds that cannot fly, kiwis can run very fast.
They can run faster than a person.
They also have very sharp nails on their claws.
These are useful when they are attacking their enemies.

Kiwis use their strong feet to burrow into the ground. During the day, they sleep in their burrows.

DID YOU KNOW?

Kiwis are the size of a hen but their eggs are six times the size of a hen's egg. Each egg is nearly the size of an emu's egg.

emu

kiwi

hen

FAST FACTS

Name: kiwi
Habitat: grasslands, forests
Diet: worms, fruit, seeds
Predators: ferrets, dogs, cats, possums, rats
Where found: New Zealand

Ostriches

Ostriches come from Africa. They are the biggest and fastest birds on land. They can run as fast as a car. Ostriches use their wings to help them change direction while running.

small wings

feathers

strong legs

sharp claw

Ostriches cannot fly because their wings are too small for the size and weight of their body.

When an ostrich is in danger, it will kick its enemy with its strong legs. It has a long sharp claw on each foot. An ostrich's kick is so strong that it can kill a lion or even a person.

The female ostrich sits on her eggs during the day and the male sits on them at night.

DID YOU KNOW?

An ostrich lays the biggest egg of any bird. It weighs as much as 24 hen's eggs.

FAST FACTS

Name: ostrich
Habitat: grasslands
Diet: grass, shrubs, seeds, roots, leaves, flowers and sometimes grasshoppers
Predators: cheetahs, lions, leopards, dogs, hyenas
Where found: Africa

Picture Glossary

camouflage

habitat

claws

hollow

diet

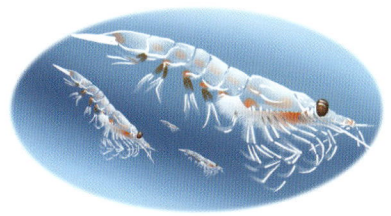

krill

dingo

nostrils

Even though penguins, emus, kiwis and ostriches can't fly, they are still birds.

These birds have many skills that help to keep them safe from their enemies, such as swimming, running, hiding and kicking.